Slim Goodbody's Inside Guide to Pets

DOGS

By Slim Goodbody

Illustrations: Ben McGinnis

Consultant: James Montgomery,
Doctor of Veterinary Medicine and
Kate Bergen Pierce, Doctor of Veterinary Medicine

Gareth Stevens
Publishing

Dedication: To Chico, my big-headed dog grandson, and to Kelly, Cloud, Graybar, Mackey, Sully, Lyda and Ebony — all who have enriched my life.

Please visit our web site at: www.garethstevens.com.
For a free color catalog describing Gareth Stevens Publishing's list
of high-quality books, call 1-800-542-2595 (USA) or 1-800-387-3178 (Canada).
Gareth Stevens Publishing's fax: 1-877-542-2596

Library of Congress Cataloging-in-Publication Data

Burstein, John.
    Dogs / John Burstein.
      p. cm. — (Slim Goodbody's inside guide to pets)
      ISBN-13: 978-0-8368-8955-0 ISBN-10: 0-8368-8955-X (lib. bdg.)
    Includes bibliographical references and index.
    1. Dogs—Juvenile literature. I. Title.
    SF426.5B86 2008
    636.7—dc22   2007033453

This edition first published in 2008 by
Gareth Stevens Publishing
A Weekly Reader® Company
1 Reader's Digest Road
Pleasantville, NY 10570-7000 USA

This edition copyright © 2008 by Gareth Stevens, Inc.
Text and artwork copyright © 2008 by Slim Goodbody Corp. (www.slimgoodbody.com).
Slim Goodbody is a registered trademark of Slim Goodbody Corp.

Photos: All photos from i Stock Photos; Skulls Unlimited International p. 8.
Illustrations: Ben McGinnis, Adventure Advertising

Managing Editor: Valerie J. Weber, Wordsmith Ink
Designer: Tammy West
Gareth Stevens Senior Managing Editor: Lisa M. Guidone
Gareth Stevens Creative Director: Lisa Donovan

Printed in the United States of America

1 2 3 4 5 6 7 8 9 10 10 09 08

CONTENTS

Words that appear in the glossary are printed in **boldface** type the first time they occur in the text.

DOGS, WONDERFUL DOGS

Hello! My name is Chico, and I am here to tell you about the greatest pets in the world — dogs. Not that there is anything wrong with rabbits, guineas pigs, birds, or fish. Even cats are okay sometimes, but dogs are the best. Can you think of any other animals that are nearly as helpful as dogs?

- There are guide dogs for the blind.
  Are there any guide rabbits?

- There are guard dogs.
  Are there any guard guinea pigs?

- There are hunting dogs.
  Are there any hunting goldfish?

There are police dogs.
Are there any police parrots?

There are fire-station dogs.
Have you ever heard of a fire-station cat?

I don't think so!

Dogs are loving, loyal, trustworthy, and hardworking. Dogs are **humanity**'s oldest friends. We have lived, worked, and played together for over twelve thousand years! The only thing we ask for in return is food, shelter, and friendship.

Chico's Tips

We dogs are happiest when we get plenty of love. Be sure to give us lots of pats and hugs every day.

There are more than four hundred different kinds of dogs. We come in hundreds of shapes, sizes, and colors.

We can be huge like a Great Dane

or tiny like a Chihuahua.

We can be thick like a mastiff

or thin like a greyhound.

We can be long like a dachshund

or short like a pug.

We can have ears that stick up or ears that drag on the ground.

We can have a solid-colored coat

or be spotted all over.

Even though we look different on the outside, inside we are the same.

Chico's Tips

If you are going to choose a dog for a pet, please choose wisely. If you live in a small apartment, you might not want a Great Dane. If you live in the city, you might not want a dog that needs a lot of space to run in like a greyhound. If you want to play hard with your dog, a toy poodle might not be your best choice. If your mom or dad hates dog hair on the furniture, you might not want a dog that sheds a lot, such as a collie. Think about the kind of dog that will be best for you **AND** your family.

MY OWN BONES

I thought it would be fun to compare our skeletons.

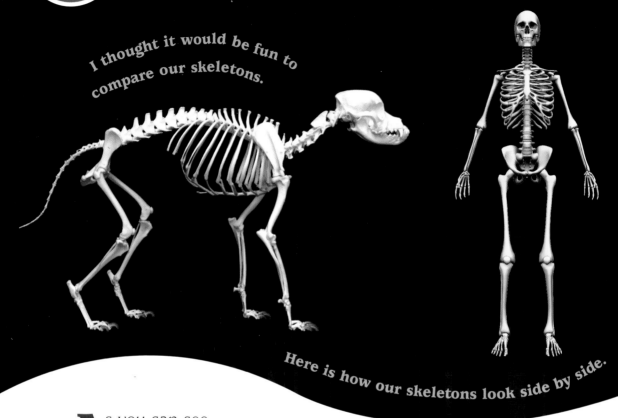

Here is how our skeletons look side by side.

As you can see, our skeletons have a lot in common. For example, we both have skull bones, neck bones, a spine, ribs, four limbs, shoulder blades, hip bones, and toe bones. Of course, one major difference is easy to see. I have bones for a tail, and you do not.

Bones do pretty much the same jobs for dogs and humans. For example, jawbones hold our teeth, skulls protect our brains, and ribs shield our heart and lungs.

Here is something you may find amazing. Dogs have over 100 more bones than people do! We have 321 bones. You have 206 bones. Some of the extra bones are in our tails and our skulls. For example, we have 35 skull bones and you have only 8.

8

DEWCLAW

FUN FACT

I have five toes just like you do. One of my toes, called a dewclaw, is too high to be useful, however. Each toe has a claw, which is actually a big toenail.

The Shape of Our Heads

Human skulls all have a similar shape. Dogs have three very differently shaped skulls:

One shape is long and narrow and can be seen in such **breeds** as collies and Russian wolfhounds.

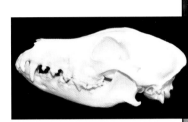

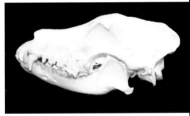

One shape is medium long and wide and is seen in breeds such as German shepherds and beagles.

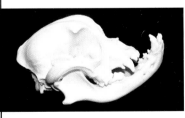

One shape is short and wide and can be seen in breeds such as Boston terriers, pugs, and English bulldogs.

Chico's Tips

Dogs need our nails clipped every couple of months. When you clip our nails, do not cut them too short. That hurts! Only clip off the clear part of the nail that sticks out past our foot pads. Adults, not children, should do the clipping.

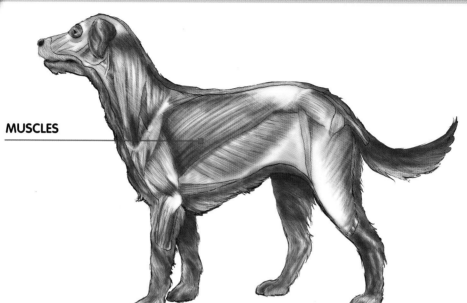

MUSCLES

Dog muscles and human muscles work the same way. For example, our neck muscles move our heads, our jaw muscles help us chew, our thigh muscles help us run and jump, and our stomach muscles protect our inner **organs**.

Of course, I have a set of muscles that you do not. I have muscles that let me lift, lower, and wag my tail.

On the Run

We also stand differently. I stand on four legs, and you stand on two. My upper body muscles support half my weight and are about as strong as my lower body muscles. Your upper body muscles do not have to hold you up. Your stronger leg muscles do that job.

My muscles make me a great runner. With four legs to work with, I can run a lot faster than you can. My muscles also help me run long distances. Of course, not all dogs are as fast as I am. For example, dogs with big heads and short legs are not so speedy.

Chico's Tips

Be sure to give your dog lots of exercise. Dogs need to run to stay healthy and keep their muscles strong.

Both dogs and humans get two sets of teeth. I get twenty-eight baby teeth and forty-two adult teeth. You get twenty baby teeth and thirty-two adult teeth. Not only do I have more teeth, they also grow in a lot faster than yours. All my baby teeth are in by the time I'm eight weeks old.

Maybe I have more teeth than you because they have more jobs to do than your teeth do. For example, you hold things with your hands. I hold things with my teeth. You use a knife to cut up food. If I want bite-sized pieces, I have to bite. In a fight, your hands are your major weapons. My teeth are my major weapons.

FUN FACT
You might think that I chew my food really well. I'll tell you a secret — I don't. Once I get a piece of food, I gulp it down as fast as I can.

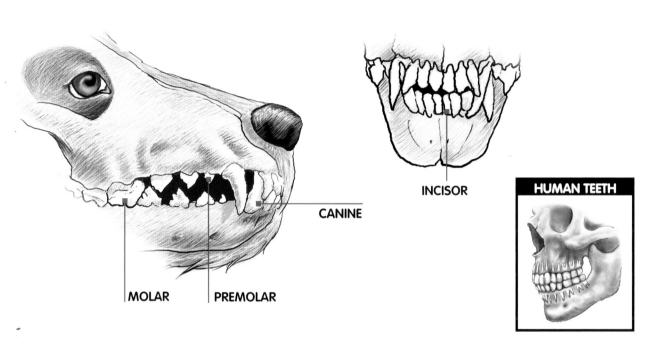

CANINE

INCISOR

HUMAN TEETH

MOLAR **PREMOLAR**

Fangs for the Food!

I have four kinds of teeth. They are called incisors, canines, premolars, and molars.

My incisors let me grab and bite something. I use them like scissors to cut through meat or to scrape meat off bones.

Sometimes called fangs, my canines are my largest, sharpest teeth. They also help me grab and hold on to something and to tear and shred meat. Canines are my best weapons. My premolars and molars can cut food, but they are mostly meant to crush and grind it.

Chico's Tips

Your dog needs to have his teeth brushed at least once a week. In between brushings, special dental treats and crunchy vegetables such as carrots will keep your dog's teeth clean.

LIKE MY FUR COAT?

I have my very own beautiful, colorful fur coat. I wear it all the time. It protects my skin and helps keep me warm on cold days. Fur is really just another name for thick hair.

Dog hair can be black, brown, red, yellow, white, or several different colors. Older dogs often grow gray hair. Dog hair can be long, medium, or short. It can feel smooth, silky, or wiry. I have dog friends with coats with all kinds of patterns — spots, patches, and stripes.

Most dogs have three basic kinds of hair:

- A soft undercoat that helps keep us warm in winter.

- Guard hairs that protect our skin and overcoat. Guard hairs are stiffer and usually longer than undercoat hairs.

- Whiskers, which are the stiff hairs on our faces. If anything brushes against our whiskers, we feel it.

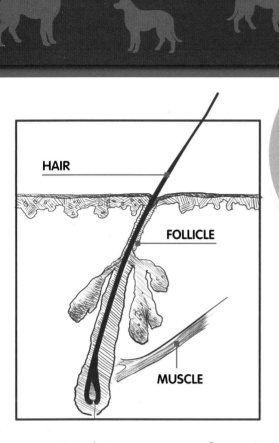

HAIR

FOLLICLE

MUSCLE

FUN FACT

Some breeds, such as poodles, have hair that keeps on growing all the time. Some dogs have very little hair, like the Mexican hairless. This dog only has hair on its head and tail.

My hair grows out from tiny holes under my skin called follicles. Each hair is connected to tiny muscles in my skin. These muscles can make my hair stand up and bristle when I am scared. These muscles also let me fluff up my coat when it is cold. Fluffing up traps a layer of warm air between my skin and the cold outdoors, keeping me warm.

When my hair reaches a certain length, it stops growing and falls out. This shedding usually starts in spring. Shedding keeps me cooler in the warm months. Then in the fall, my coat grows thicker and longer.

Chico's Tips

Brush your dog's hair at least once a week. Dogs with long or thick coats need brushing more often than short-haired dogs. Brushing gets rid of dead hair and helps keep her skin healthy.

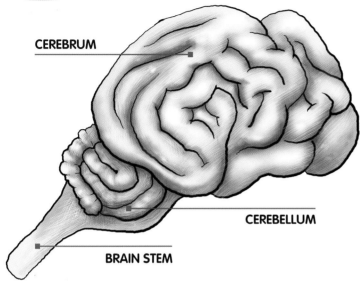

CEREBRUM

CEREBELLUM

BRAIN STEM

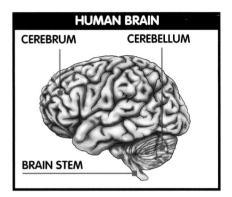

HUMAN BRAIN

CEREBRUM   CEREBELLUM

BRAIN STEM

My brain looks a lot like yours. It has the same parts — a cerebrum, a **cerebellum**, and a **brain stem**. Like your brain, my brain gets information from my senses. Dogs have the same five senses as humans. Some of my senses work better than yours and some do not. My brain is smaller than yours, however, and cannot think in all the ways that your brain can.

I am still smart, though. Many scientists believe that the ability to learn is a sure sign of intelligence. If that is true, I am one brainy beast. I have learned to follow commands like "sit," "stay," and "come." I have learned how to escape from a yard. I have learned to find my way home. I have learned the best ways to steal food. Oops, please don't tell anyone that.

A Talking Tail

Another sign of intelligence is the ability to communicate. I yip, bark, whimper, growl, and howl. Each of these sounds means something. I whimper if I am hurt or afraid. I bark if I am happy, want attention, or hear something strange. I growl if I am afraid or angry. If I show my teeth without growling, I am ready to attack and bite. I howl if I want to let far-away dogs know where I am.

I can also communicate with my tail. If I am holding my tail high and wagging it, I'm feeling happy. If I drop my tail and stay still, I'm uneasy or worried. If I pull my tail between my legs, I am afraid.

Chico's Tips

If you are teaching your dog a trick or a new command, give her a chance to rest every ten minutes or so. Our brains do not learn well unless we have time to play and relax.

SWELL SMELL

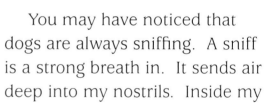

My sense of smell is at least fifty times better than yours. Imagine you can smell a stinky sock that is 1 foot (.3 meters) away from you. I can smell that same stinky sock from 50 feet (15 m) away! Some scientists think dogs can smell 1 million times better than people. If they can, I could smell that sock from 1 million feet (304,800 m) away!

You may have noticed that dogs are always sniffing. A sniff is a strong breath in. It sends air deep into my nostrils. Inside my nostrils, I have about 220 million **nerve endings** that **detect** smells. (You have only about 5 to 10 million of these nerve endings in your nose). They pick up odors and send information about them to my brain. The part of my brain that receives smell messages is forty times bigger than the same part in your brain!

Nose on the News

I love to sniff everything. I sniff the air, the ground, trees, buildings, and just about everything else. Smell brings me the neighborhood news. It tells me what people, dogs, cats, and other animals have been around. It lets me know if any of my buddies are nearby.

Our sense of smell also lets us help you in emergencies. Rescue dogs can track down somebody who is lost. They can also find people who are trapped in a building that has fallen down.

Not all dog noses are the same. Some of us have a better sense of smell than others. For example, if you have a choice, you might not want to choose this short-nosed guy to track somebody down.

FUN FACT
The outside of my nose is a little wet. This wetness helps trap odors.

Chico's Tips

Dogs love the smell of food, and we will gobble down whatever we can. Please do not over-feed us. Puppies need to eat three or four times a day until they are about six months old. Once we are grown, we probably need just two meals each day. If we eat more than that, we might grow too fat, which is not healthy.

19

LISTEN HEAR

Sometimes I start barking in the middle of the night, and my owner cannot understand why. I usually don't bark because I am sad and want company. I bark because I hear a sound — one that my owner can't hear. Dogs have better sense of hearing than people do. Dogs can hear sounds from about four times farther away than people can. For example, if a bird is singing in the woods, you may not be able to hear it until you are 100 yards (91 m) away from it. I can hear the same bird song from 400 yards (366 m) away. I can easily hear special dog whistles that make sounds too high for human ears to hear.

Chico's Tips
Make sure to keep your dog's ears clean. You can use a wet washcloth to do the job. Please do not rub too hard.

Ears on the Move

One of the reasons I can hear so well is that I have fifteen different muscles that can turn my outer ears in all directions. I can turn one ear one way and the other ear another way. I feel a little sorry for you humans. You only have six outer ear muscles, so you can hardly move your ears at all.

My ear movements allow me to pick up sounds very quickly. I can locate a sound in .06 seconds. When a sound comes, my outer ear sends it down my ear canal to my eardrum. My eardrum vibrates and sends the message on to special nerves in my inner ear. These nerves then send the information to my brain.

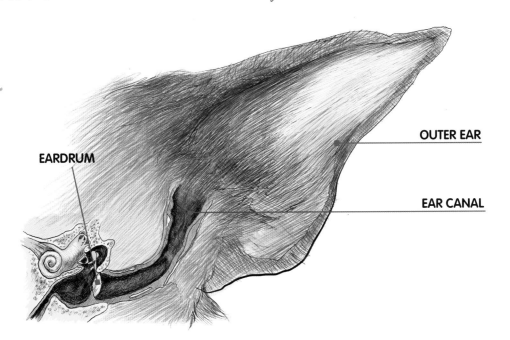

EARDRUM

OUTER EAR

EAR CANAL

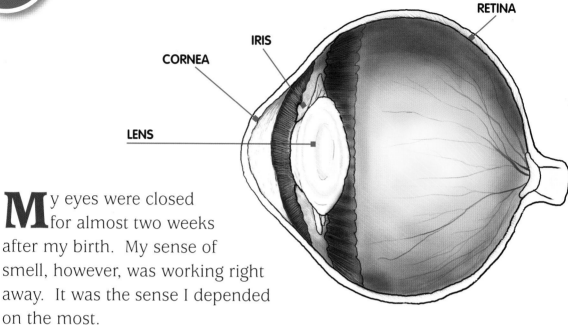

RETINA

IRIS

CORNEA

LENS

My eyes were closed for almost two weeks after my birth. My sense of smell, however, was working right away. It was the sense I depended on the most.

Human eyes and dog eyes work pretty much the same way. They both have a lens, cornea, iris, and retina. There are also nerves at the back of our eyes. When we see something, these nerves send information to our brains.

If I compare my sense of sight to yours, I would say that mine is better in some ways and worse in other ways. For example:

- In dim light, I can see things better than you can.

- In bright light, you can see things better than I can.

- I see things that are off to the side better because my eyes are set farther apart than yours are.

- You see things in front of you better because your eyes are set closer together.

- I can see some colors. You can see more colors.

- If something is moving, I can see it better than you can.

- If something is at rest, you can see it better than I can.

One other thing I think is pretty cool. I am a lot shorter than you, so I see things from lower down than you do. Imagine your eyes were at the same height as mine. What would the world look like to you then?

Chico's Tips
As dogs grow older, our eyesight sometimes gets weaker. Be sure to have a **vet** check your dog's eyes at least once a year.

If you see food that looks or smells rotten, you won't eat it. If I see or smell rotten food — **YUM!** I gulp first and ask questions later! The way I figure it, the smellier the better.

You can blame this on my sense of taste, which is not as good as yours. I only have one-sixth the amount of taste buds you have. Poor me, I guess I will just have to eat that garbage!

Most of my taste buds are just in the tip of my tongue. They are located under the bumps in the tongue. They are nerve endings that send information to the brain.

LOCATION OF MOST TASTE BUDS

Tongues As Tools

My tongue is helpful in other ways. I use it to push food to the back of my mouth and down my throat. I use it to lick my coat clean and to lick my friends.

When I am hot, I hang my tongue out and pant. The water on my tongue **evaporates** into the air and cools me off. When your skin sweats, the water also evaporates to cool you off. I can't get rid of body heat as quickly as you do, however. That's why my owner makes sure I never get too hot. For example, I am never left inside a car with the windows closed on a warm day.

Chico's Tips

Some foods are bad for your dog, even if they taste good. Chemicals in chocolate can speed up your dog's heart and cause real trouble. Fatty foods like ham, pork, and bacon are hard for him to digest. Milk can also upset his stomach, and avocados can actually send your dog to the pet hospital!

Iam a pet who loves to be petted. I think it is sort of strange that the word *pet* has two meanings. A pet is an animal you love, and a pet is also a soft pat you give your pet.

I love it when my owner pets me. I love lying down next to my friends and snuggling. I have nerve endings all over my body that detect touch, even on my paws. These nerve endings send nice feelings right to my brain.

FUN FACT

As you know, dogs cannot talk. Sometimes we use touch to express our feelings. When I lie down close to my owner, I am saying, "I love you."

Touch was the first sense I had. When puppies are born, they cannot see or hear. It takes more than a week for their sight and hearing to start working. That means touch was super important those first few days. Touch let me know my mom was around.

Chico's Tips

Pat your dog a million times a day. If you can't do that, can you make it a thousand?

27

AMAZING FACTS

I hope you've had fun learning about dogs. Of course, we have only "scratched" the surface. There is really no end to the things I could tell you, but my owner just set out a delicious bone for me to chew. While I'm busy with my bone, here are some amazing facts that you can chew on!

- A dog was the first living creature sent into space. Her name was Laika. She was launched into space on November 3, 1957.

- The oldest dog on record was Bluey, an Australian cattle dog, that died at the age of twenty-nine.

- The heaviest dog on record, an English Mastiff, weighs in at 286 pounds (130 kilograms). That's about the same weight as a black bear!

- The tallest dog is a Great Dane. Measured from the ground to its shoulder, it's 42.2 inches (107 centimeters) tall. It's about as tall as a male lion.

- The smallest dog on record was a matchbox-sized Yorkshire terrier owned by Arthur Marples of Blackburn, England. This tiny creature, which died in 1945 at the age of nearly two years, stood 2 ½ inches (6.3 cm) tall at the shoulder and measured 3 ½ inches (8.9 cm) from the tip of it's nose to the base of its tail.

The fastest dog in the world is probably the greyhound. The speediest greyhound can run almost 45 miles (72 kilometers) per hour. Only cheetahs run faster.

Dogs spend a great deal of time sleeping — about ten to sixteen hours a day.

Tile **mosaics** meaning "Beware the Dog" have been found on doorsteps in ancient Roman cities.

People in ancient China stayed warm by carrying small dogs in their sleeves.

Chow-chow dogs have blue-black tongues.

Labrador retrievers were originally bred to haul fishing nets out of the water.

Saur was a dog that became the "king" of Norway for three years during the eleventh century. The Norwegian king was angry because his subjects wanted to get rid of him. He placed his dog Saur on the throne and demanded that the people treat the dog like a king.

GLOSSARY

ancestors — animals from whom an individual or group is descended

ancient — relating to a time long ago

brain stem — the part of the brain that controls the inner workings of the body, such as how fast the heart beats and how much air the body needs

breeds — different groups of animals that share the same features

cerebellum — the part of the brain that controls movement and balance

cerebrum — the part of the brain that receives messages from the sense nerves

detect — to discover or find out information

evaporates — turns into a gas and disappears into the air

humanity — a group made up of all human beings in the world

mosaics — pictures or designs made by setting small pieces of glass, tile, or stone of different colors into another material

nerve endings — the parts of nerves that detect information about the world and send that information to the brain

organs —parts of the body, such as the heart, lungs, stomach, or liver, that do specific jobs

sacred — very special and worthy of being worshipped; holy

vet — short for *veterinarian*, a doctor who takes care of animals

FOR MORE INFORMATION

BOOKS

A Dog's Best Friend: An Activity Book for Kids and Their Dogs. Lisa Rosenthal (Chicago Review Press)

Everything Dog: What Kids Really Want to Know About Dogs. Kids' FAQs (series). Marty Crisp (Northword Press)

Puppy. ASPCA Pet Care Guides (series). Mark Evans (DK Children)

Puppy Training for Kids. Sarah Whitehead (Barron's Educational Series)

WEB SITES

American Kennel Club: Kids' Corner
www.akc.org/public_education/kids_corner/kidscorner.cfm
This online newsletter features stories about responsible dog ownership and information about dogs' behavior and bodies.

ASPCA Animaland Pet Care
www.aspca.org/site/PageServer?pagename = kids_pc_dog_411
Find out basic facts about dogs and how to care for them. You can also click on a link to watch Pet Care Cartoons.

Fact Monster: Pets
factmonster.info/pets.html
Scroll down to find articles on dogs on this site, which has information about many kinds of pets.

How to Love Your Dog
www.loveyourdog.com
Click on links to find out more about dogs' bodies and how to care for a dog.

INDEX

ABOUT THE AUTHOR

John Burstein (also known as Slim Goodbody) has been entertaining and educating children for over thirty years. His programs have been broadcast on CBS, PBS, Nickelodeon, USA, and Discovery. He has won numerous awards including the Parent's Choice Award and the President's Council's Fitness Leader Award. Currently, Mr. Burstein tours the country with his multimedia live show "Bodyology." For more information, please visit slimgoodbody.com.